TABOO
By
Thomas Piggott

Contents

COMMAND CENTRAL

The brain is our primary control centre, a fantastically complex organ containing billions of nerves that can simultaneously process information from our bodies, operate our internal organs, generate thoughts and emotions, store and recall memories and control movement.

Information is transferred from short-term memory to long-term memory, it is a bit like a sorting centre. It lets you think, dream, reason and experience emotions. My past is always haunting me. All my mistakes and bad choices, I can never forget them. I wish I had a way to delete really bad memories from my brain. Sometimes when I sleep, is the time my brain decides to revisit all of my bad memories and visions.

INTRODUCTION

This is my true story on how an innocent child can be sexually abused by a respected adult with authority that will lead to far, far more than you would wish on anyone. From early days to depression to a mental health hospital, all because my childhood days had taken a turn for the worst. It is about my life and the person I could have been. Broken relationships, family feuds and losing many good friends due to my behaviour.

I will title my book *Taboo* as in not to be spoken about. At that time, years ago, what happened to me could not be real or understood as it would appear you were liar or just seeking attention. The very thought of trying to tell anyone, even my family, made me weep. Would anyone believe me? As I write this book I will let you into my feelings and also state some basic facts that many people are not aware of, reaching out to you to read and listen and learn.

My aim for writing this is to take away the silent burden that I have carried with me into adult life but to also make you understand what it is like to have something taken away from you. Heaven forbid, I hope you do not see these signs in any of your family, so maybe my thoughts and words will help. Thinking back, I wish and hoped that someone would have noticed that something was not right. This has taken two years for me to write as it was not easy for me to open up my memory box. I guess if it was a story of romance or fiction it would be easier to write, so hey-ho here it goes. I am being deliberate in you getting to know me before the hurt comes.

I have always felt that I could write a book, I think there is an unwritten book inside most of us. I just needed some motivation to write mine. Now I hope I have fulfilled my dream and can be at peace knowing that if you're reading this book, then I have got your attention.

It has always felt to me that a fear of judgement is the mark of guilt and the burden of insecurity. I was never sure how best to carry it, too heavy for a child. Trying to avoid the pain associated with my memory I suffered in silence, my childhood was stolen. Sometimes things that get stolen are returned to you, but this one is not wanted back.

Indeed, it has often occurred to me that any man is potentially only a few small steps away from utter ruination. Redundancy, leading to drinking, causing a marriage to break down, resulting in losing my home and my dignity and friends. Yes, all of this happened to me. I will try to breakdown all of this in different chapters but all of these topics do have a link.

Avoiding the road to unhappiness is not going to lead you to the road of happiness. I need to travel along the unhappiness to get where I am now. If I do not do this journey I would not find myself again. It would be nice to be loved again for who I am now and not the way I was.

CHAPTER ONE- CHILDHOOD DAYS

Reaching out to you. For every person that feels too afraid to know what will be ridiculed, find someone you really trust, respects you and will accept you for who you are. I never did that or had that opportunity to do that as in my childhood days it was unimaginable and hard for anyone to react as if it was for real, so it became a taboo a do not talk about it situation because it is just a fantasy that you have made up and is not heard of or possible. People listen now but back then it was hard to express your feelings to anyone. It was always there inside me, the truth is real but making it real to other people is very difficult, like a brick wall that I would hit my head on many times. Hiding under the bed to make the world go away. To this single day I have not had one person say I am sorry I just could not believe you or accept it could happen. Ouch!

As I did, please do not think you are alone, reach out, the world is a better place and no not everything happens for a reason. My story is that you can get your life back with self-respect and tell yourself it was not your fault. I was too young to realise it was wrong.

I was born in Birmingham, UK. My parents lived in Ireland but at the time there were no jobs available so they got the boat to move to England to seek employment and a council home. My early days were okay but I had a bit of a temperament and temper and was always getting into trouble and fights. My dad was not the type of person you would associate with the caring dads these days. He never taught me anything or even seemed to care. Mostly he would sit in the kitchen on his own as if he was a stranger. These days you have loving parents that want the best for you, hug you, watch out for you, help you with your homework and love you very much. I have to admit I was naughty and maybe deserved my punishment. I had many beatings from my dad's belt and even a cricket stump smashed on my shins; that really hurt. I would go and hide under my bed. Sometimes I never made it to my bed as for being naughty I was locked in the kitchen cupboard for a few hours to teach me a lesson. That did not really bother me, sad to say that I felt safe in there. I felt that I deserved it.

At the time I really did not know right from wrong. Just an innocent child learning from my mistakes. There was nothing I could do about it and it was just a part of growing up. If only one person who reads my true story can look out for the tell-tale signs in your children then I will have achieved something. This does not mean you have to be over cautious but just to check the smile on my face is not hiding the hurt in my eyes.

In those days our home was next to the Birmingham City Football ground. Sometimes I would climb fences just to see what all the crowd and noise was about as I had never kicked a football before, never mind even owning one. This was about to get me into even more trouble. One of the benefits of living next to the football stadium was that on match days many people would park their cars on my road before going into the stadium. There was always plenty of space on our road to park a car as most of us were too poor to own a car never mind learning how to drive one legally. I seized my opportunity in anticipation on match days to watch the cars park up. It was not the best of areas at the time and prone to people breaking into cars to get whatever they could. It was not uncommon for a man of family and children to return to their car after the game was over, only to find that one of the car windows had been smashed in. This led to me looking at the cars that were parking up on our road and walking over to the driver and asking them if they wanted me to look after their car while they were in the stadium. Most people said yes and I got a few pence for each car I watched. This caused many fights chasing off youths that were looking for something to steal. As mentioned I had a bad temper so when needed I always found myself fighting above my weight.

There were many scraps but one day always sticks in my mind. It was a football match day so I eagerly awaited the cars to park up so I could get my few pence reward per car in the knowledge that I was doing some good and also getting some money to spend on sweets in the corner shop. On this particular day another boy from one of the neighbouring terrace houses had seen what I was doing and decided to get a bit of the action, so to speak. This was a threat to my territory and my idea. Thinking back, I am not proud of what I did but let's just say he had a bloody nose and a black eye. This made the situation worse as his mum was a huge lady, came out of their door to confront me. My mother heard the commotion and came outside to see what was happening. As a caring mum, she stood up for me.

The lad's mum was not in the mood to listen so pushed my mum through the front glass window. Of course she had cuts and bruises and spent the night in hospital. My fault and I really blamed myself and thought now is the time for me to really grow up and be good. On the downside it led me to be tamed and open to vultures as you will read later on. I became easy meat with no idea other than this must be normal behaviour and is a consequence for my behaviour.

How could an adult treat a child in such a bad way, so I guess this must be normal and happened to other children? I did not have the strength to resist because at the time I was not sure if this was right or wrong, or maybe just a learning period as a reward for the treats I was given. I was pretty much fearless as a child. In the summer I would go outside to our garden with a jar and collect bees that were around, the bigger the better. I would release them after an hour.

There is always a stage in everyone's life when they realise that they don't have to put up with anything that has been done to them as a child, if they don't want to they can do something about it.

CHAPTER TWO- SCHOOL DAYS

In my school days I did some good things and some bad things but it was another journey in my life that had many challenges and taught me more than school lessons. I would get two pence each morning for a bus fare. Most days I chose to walk and save the money for the school tuck shop as a treat to myself. Not like today with all the roads full of traffic with mothers and fathers doing the school run and dropping the kids off on the way to work. That may seem a bit over-protective but at least they know their children are safe for the day and not open to any danger.

I remember on my walk home after school this strange man, who seemed very kind, stopped to talk to me and would give me a few pence. I guess I was being groomed for his next victim. Not sure why but I did not like him very much and he smelled and stank so I chose to walk a different way after school to avoid him. Looking back on my memory of this it makes me think, what is wrong with people and society that they end up like this. Was it because they were abused as a child and decided it was payback time, how sick is that? As you will find out later in my book it made me a stronger person and not a low-life that would stoop to that unthinkable, cowardly and wrong behaviour.

Anyway, back to my school days. My infant school was normal enough before my progress to junior school. Most of all, my teacher wanted us to read books and sometimes stand up and recite a paragraph. Learning to read and write is very important to your future life. Even at my age the books became too easy to read and I guess I was learning how to speed read, not good if you really want to relax and enjoy the book.

There was a bookcase in our classroom that held all the books that we would read and understand what the book was about. In my first year I had read and understood every one of them to the extent that all the other kids were still reading and there was not another book left for me to read so I just sat there in silence. How can a young child decide their learning capability? I did, so I asked my mother to move me to another school, which she did and it turned out to be an educational and happy time in my younger days.

My new junior school was a catholic one and very strict but it was just what I needed. My mind was focused on learning without realising at the time, that it would drive me to achieve a better life when my school days were over.

People are always judging you based on where you are from, where you went to school, how you look, how you talk. But at the end of the day, you're going to look in the mirror and accept who you are. It is all about being authentic.

I did not really like my first school, even at my age, the method of teaching did not feel right and I sensed it was not really helping me. Some schools and teachers these days take pride in their work and look to achieve targets that will improve the school and attract more parents to think that this is where I want to send my child to learn and listen and get a good education. Being accepted for a school place you need to list your three preferences but further more you are required to live within a one mile area, called the catchment area. My next junior school was even worse because the teachers taught us in a different way to the extent it would not sink in or we would not be able to learn or progress from it. It was time for me to ask my mother to allow me to move schools again. She wanted the best for us so found me a school namely Corpus Christi.

This was more like it, good teachers, educational and also strict. It was about passing my exams, making new friends and also kicking a football for the first time. Most of us at the time would see our school days as a chore and could not wait for the end of the lessons bell to ring. Now a lot of us think it was one of the best things in their lives and would say they wished they could go back to that time in their life again.

What's amazing is, if young people understand how doing well in school makes the rest of their life so much interesting, they would be more motivated. It is so far away in time that they can't appreciate what it means for the whole of their life.

CHAPTER THREE- CHILD ABUSE

This is the most difficult part of writing my book from pen to paper. It has not been about tears at bedtime but more about tears in the daytime. It has taken me a long time to write this due to my teardrops and putting my pen down on the table, going to bed and hiding under my duvet to make this reality in my life go away.

His name is or was Jeffrey Davis. One of the few things I have in my life that I have left is my sense of humour. That is one thing that nobody can take away from me. To finally face this memory that never went away from me and begin to accept that it really happened, that it was like a bolt of lightning that zapped me. My life as I had known it was about to change for the worse.

Child sex abuse exists but some people believe that the accused is not capable of such a crime. It is not unheard of for parents to support the suspect at this time as it is too unimaginable to believe that what I was trying to say is actually the truth. It is not easy for someone to come forward and tell you about the abuse, apart from where it will lead to. Your humiliation at revealing and opening up your bad memory could lead to depression and mental health problems after letting open the dark side of your brain. This happened with me and the shining light at the end of the tunnel was never found. Often there is no physical evidence and no witnesses, only my allegation that molestation occurred.

It all started not long after my father decided to walk out on my brother and two sisters and left us all to fend for ourselves. His parting words to me were "You are a bad boy and will spend most of your life in prison."

I certainly proved him wrong on that comment and began to think I was now the eldest man in the household. I was not unhappy to see him walk away from us; it was more of a relief. If my mother ever went out at a weekend with a friend or neighbour he would always be standing in the window peeking out of the curtains waiting for her to return home. He never went out much to bars or pubs to associate with friends. I don't think he really had any friends. Once the door was opened and my mother was at home I could hear her footsteps on the stairs. I never liked to go to sleep until she was home safe and sound.

That was when so many bad things were about to happen and they continued every Saturday night until he left us in peace. He would question and taunt my mother about if she was chatting to another man while out with her friend, had she kissed anybody or danced with anybody. It got so loud that we could not sleep until the ranting was over. My mother took a lot of beatings from him while lying in bed at night ready to go to sleep and trying to put the day behind her. This was not to be as the slaps and punches continued.

That is when I decide enough is enough and on each weekend when it started I would run in to their front bedroom and jump in between them to make it stop. I never gave up and continued to do this at the expense of my father giving me a few slaps. On occasions in the morning, when no one was in the kitchen he would give me a few more slaps and tell me never to go into their bedroom again. I decided to ignore that and continued to go in there if I heard something, shouting and more slaps. I thought he was a reclusive, mild-mannered man but his temper got the better of him. I will never know what his childhood was like but guessed it must have been related in some way. I never got to know him really well which is sad for a father and son.

I started to feel free and did well at my new grammar school. I was becoming a happy boy and found love for football and became very good at it. By chance, or maybe not by chance I was spotted playing for my school football team. After the game a man called Mr Davis approached me and asked if I wanted to play for his Sunday football team. He seemed like a nice genuine man to the fact that he drove me home to ask for my mother's permission. I just thought my life was getting better, playing for my school team and also playing for a Sunday team in a proper organised league. I had also made some new friends in my team mates.

I was only about eleven or twelve years of age but I began to notice the extra attention I was getting. After mid-week training he would offer to give me a lift home, I accepted this. All my other team mates had mothers or fathers that would be waiting outside to take their kids home.

I also became aware that we were told to have a shower in the changing room after football practice and that I was getting special attention. Davis would be waiting with a towel for me to dry off but also would be staring at my private parts. Is that right or wrong, I just assumed that it was to make sure I was clean and had a proper shower and wash. Week by week he would continue to take me home after training or football matches to gain the trust of my mother. My mum was the type of person that would welcome conversation with a smile on her face. Now I can understand why she did not think anything was wrong because although Davis was not a well-dressed man, maybe he thought he was due to wearing a suit and this came across as confident. He had a good manner of speaking and after all he was my football coach, looking out for me. It was the ideal opportunity for him to groom me, from a broken home, no father figure, I was ripe and easily liked the attention I was being given.

I could stay at home every night, take cold showers every day and throw my life away. I didn't steal and I didn't lie but I could feel and I could cry. In fact you may not understand that for a boy or man to cry in public is not what I wanted to do.

He had a red tatty rusty van in which we were about to begin our journeys in. I remind you that at the time I was a lonely, lost child that felt unwanted so the attention I was about to get was new to me. I did not know at the time how wrong it was and how it would affect me in later life. I loved having the football at my feet and trying to be the best on the pitch, a lot of the times I was about to achieve that, due to my desire to play football. The obvious thing for Davis to do was ask me to go to a live professional football match with him. By now he had my trust and I was being spoilt and I was going to paid games that other parents could not afford to pay for. It was exciting times. We went to Nottingham, Coventry, Wolverhampton, Derby, Leicester and many more other stadiums that any boy at my age could only dream about.

Once I was hooked on this new found life the next stage was for Davis to start taking me out for meals. It was not your McDonalds or Burger King but proper restaurants like La' reserve or anywhere with a posh name and a nice menu. I guess other customers at other tables must have thought how innocent it was and that my dad (dread the thought) had taken me out for a meal. Why did I not see that this was all wrong and why would he be doing this? So I was getting to go to football matches and nice restaurants so I wonder to this day why none of my family or friends questioned why I was getting all this special treatment.

Moving on from the meals and football the next stage was to go to the cinema to watch a movie. Most of the times it was to watch a movie that I had never heard of or was any good. I guess it was his way and he was probably not interested in the movie. It was his time to have his wicked moments. He always smelt greasy with bad body odour. Always with shoes, trousers and mainly a brown blazer, I suppose he looked the part as a normal type of guy, no questions asked.

I have fallen apart and cried for a few days trying to complete this chapter but if I continue I can fly away. It was now that the terrible things were about to happen. I know now why he picked the movie times at a part of the day where it would be virtually empty. Sitting there in a dark cinema with no witnesses in sight. The first time it really hurt as I was only about to come to terms that my penis was not just for pissing out of. Davis then began to undo the buttons and zip on my trousers and play with my private parts, I have no memory if I ever got a hard on as I thought he was just playing with a toy that was part of me while watching the movie. I was never aroused or enjoyed it so just thought it was normal behaviour. At my age it was all new and I did not notice or think it was wrong. I was just watching the movie, eating my popcorn and let it happen.

The next movie the opposite was about to occur. Davis would say that I have played with your penis toy so it is your turn to play with mine while we are watching the movie. I could not bear the thought of undoing his trousers so he undid them himself and took my hand and put it on his penis. Now it was time to jerk and erect him until this cream like substance exploded into my hands. Then he would hand me a tissue to wipe my hands.

There were times when we did not stay to watch the movie, his filthy and twisted mind had got the pleasure it was looking for. This would happen many, many times and to this day I cannot remember all the movies we watched other than a James Bond one that was fascinating.

On the journey home from the cinema he would never talk about the disgusting filth that had just happened. Maybe he felt too guilty to talk about it. What possibly goes through a pervert and abusers mind you can never really tell but later in this book I will try to explain it the best I can.

All of the above was nothing compared to what was about to happen next. His old rusty red van was to be his torture chamber. Was this happening to me because I was a bad boy or was it because I was a good boy and this was my special treat? You have to understand that I had no idea at the time that this was so, so badly wrong for an adult to do to a boy, it was not like I was being punished for anything because I had done nothing wrong in my eyes.

Sometimes after training or football games he would drive me out to secluded places so that it did not look suspicious for him to park his van there. This was the time I was about to really feel the pain from inside that will haunt me forever. These days they would call you a pillow biter but for me it was not a choice. Pillow biting is to dull the pain. I was at this stage, sad and lonely and welcomed a fatherly cuddle. I was fully awake, some invisible alarm bell sounding in my head, unable to work out what was happening or what was expected of me. Why was I now naked and shivering in the back of a van? What was he going to do? I don't think I felt exactly afraid because I still trusted him at this stage. I was more puzzled and apprehensive, anxious to do the right thing and not upset him. But I remember desperately wanting to put my trousers back on, feeling awkward and vulnerable without any clothes. There was nowhere to run or hide as the van was locked from the inside. I stayed as still as I could, holding my breath, letting him do whatever he wanted, waiting to see what would happen next, hoping it would all be over soon.

He made me touch his penis and masturbate him which was horrible, then started to pin me down on the old carpet that was in the back of the van and forced me to do things that hurt and frightened me. Conveniently there was a pillow that was now covering my head to stifle the sounds when I cried out in fear and pain. He would press down so hard I was sure I would suffocate. Eventually I would have to give in and fall quiet as I struggled to breathe. It was very terrifying as I struggled to stay calm and become less aware of what he was doing to me. He soon moved onto other things, hold me in a grip, forcing his penis into my backside, making me cry out with pain. I didn't like what was happening to me, but I didn't think I had any option other than to let him do whatever he chose.

I felt like a piece of meat that he could do whatever he wanted with. I wasn't Tommy anymore, just an object, and that he didn't care about me as a person at all.

****

I was now his toy to play with. My arse had been sore for a few days. I dreaded the call to my bedroom to say that Mr Davis is outside waiting to take you to the pictures, have a nice time. Little did my family know that this was not about to be a nice time. I know it was wrong but felt that nobody would believe me if said I did not want to go because he was bumming me.

Eventually there was a time when my body, mind, heart and soul could not take any more. I was dropped home after another lovely evening, excuse my sarcasm, deciding to pluck up the courage to tell my mother that Mr Davis is playing with my willy and I want it to stop. I could barely get the words out of my mouth and could not reveal the full story and events. My mother looked shocked and I sensed she was not sure if to believe me or not. Then it did stop, I had my dignity back again, although an extremely bruised one that I had to try and shut it away.

The next day Davis dropped me off from training and told me my mom had called to his house and said leave my son alone, take me instead. That was very brave of her but of course he declined. So that was that, but thinking back it was not the right thing to do. The right thing should have been to call the police and let them deal with it. I dread to think who his next victim would be because that phone call was never made, so basically he had got away with it and free to move on to his next prey. I may have had no voice and no choice when I was younger, but now I do.

Everyone has to have somewhere they feel safe and there is nowhere in the real world I could do that for long. If I shut out everyone and everything else, I could finally relax. I was content when I was in a daydream most of the time, but sometimes I would be wide awake in a dream.

So much torture and pain and abuse could have been prevented if only people spoke out. As boys you are naïve to people in authority and think whatever happens to you was meant to be. How can a boy fully understand those moments in time and put a stop to it. I was just an easy target that a sick disgusting adult took advantage of. What could I do, what could I say, what can I do to explain to anyone what was happening to me, I was young and vulnerable. Just like a small animal in the wildlife that gets devoured by a bigger animal for their daily food, hopeless to run for cover or hide in the trees so you can for live another day. Fight or flight, deal with it now because tomorrow it will still be there. I did get to live for another day but knowing that my predator was still out there looking for me. To get his fix and let me live for another day knowing that I was now his pet.

When someone is feeling vulnerable they need to have their pain acknowledged, not to be made to feel worse for having it.

After all this, there were other thoughts that I would hide and not discuss with anyone. The scab that was to form on my knee from scraping it on the van floor through trying to take some of the pressure away from the pain in my bum. The scab would open and weep a few days later, it could not weep as much as I was, to be replaced by a permanent scar that I still have until this day to represent an unwanted memory. I have at times tried to cut and remove it that caused bleeding but it is with me now forever as a reminder of my child Abuse. My underwear that horrible day were innocent White clean Y fronts never to be worn again. I shut myself in my bedroom at home and cut and ripped them to shreds with tears in my eyes. I could not bring myself to tell any family my reasons why. The next day I placed them in my school uniform pocket and disposed of them in a bin.

CHAPTER FOUR- FOOTBALL YEARS

My escape now was to concentrate on my football which was all I ever wanted anyway. Davis was still my football manager but he was never to touch me again. The relief of being back to a happy child helped me with my football skills. Each year at school I would always win the one hundred metres or two hundred metre races on sports days so I knew I could run fast, maybe I should have run faster to get away from his clutches.

The team I played for was EVFC which had some good players. I found it so easy to run past the defenders and score goals. At the time, the referee handed out the Man of the Match award, or Boy of the Match award if you like. I received many of these. Our local paper, called the Sports Argus, had a page every weekend with small reports on junior football. I was to see my name on this page many times and would cut them out and create my own scrapbook, which I still have.

There were a lot of teams and hundreds of players in our football league so I was surprised to be told that I had been chosen to represent the county football team. I felt in awe of the other players that had been chosen, I had played against them for their teams in our division. I recognised them and they were very good, but I felt that maybe I was not good enough for this level. I was lacking in confidence. I was wrong to think that as on my debut I rounded two defenders and shot the ball from twenty yards, it ended up in the top left hand corner of the net giving the goalkeeper no chance. These were good times but they were about to end at the end of the season.

Davis arranged to enter a football tournament in Bruges, Belgium, also featuring a team from Holland. I was never really sure where the money came from to get us there and for our overnight stay. This was taking my football skills to a higher level to play against teams from another country and learn from it. We won both matches and felt proud of ourselves. We had bonded as a team and that would stand us good when our new season kicked off. This was never to happen as the team folded and did not register for the new season.

After the tournament we went back to our dormitory style room to have something to eat and then sleep before starting our journey back the next day. Davis had his own separate room and did approach me to sleep in there with him. I said no as I was not about to let that happen again. Why did I not tell the other boys in my team what he was like and what had happened to me. We were all too young to understand that kind of behaviour. I was to find out the following morning that another boy had said yes to sharing his room, like a special treat. I do not know what happened to him that night but seeing the tears in his eyes at breakfast I knew it would have been the same for him as it was for me. I wish now that maybe I could have prevented it but chose to stay silent, I wish I could turn back the clock and been wiser but I was still getting to grips with my own turmoil.

On our return, Davis announced that our football club was no longer to be and we were free to join any other team. Thinking back now he would have known he would not get away with it for much longer so he decided to move away. Also as the treasurer of the league he stole all the money from the league to set up his new life, he was never found.

It was in our final game as a club playing against St. Andrew's Athletic that I had another good game and even scored a hat-trick. When the game was over their manager approached me, knowing that our team was now folded, asking me if I would like to register and play with his team. I was a bit apprehensive at first; he was a short man who was bald and seemed a bid dodgy and enthusiastic to get my signature. I felt uneasy about it. I got in his car and he drove me home to seek approval from my mother. She said yes so I said yes ok. The next weekend we had an early season friendly and he handed me his address and told me to bring my kit and call at his house so that he could introduce me to my new team players.

It turned out that he was a nice family man with kids of his own so I was happy to join the team. Sometimes after the games he would ask me to come and join his family and have a seat at the table and sit down for Sunday lunch. It was a nice family and I felt happy and relaxed in their company and could now feel content that the main reason I was there was to be a part of a football team and not for some sad slimy pervert trying to get into my pants. Our final contact with Davis was to be an end of season father versus sons football match. This was to be a fun challenge. All the other boys had dads who would play in this game but I was the only one that did not have one in my life for some reason. Davis would play on the dad's team acting like he was my parent. I dread to think what the other parents thought at the time.

None of my family ever came to watch me play football but for that one day my mum came to watch me play. Maybe she was just looking out for me but I played a very good game with the thought that she was there for me, cheering from the side lines. It gave me total confidence in my ability. Who knew how I would have prospered if I had a real dad encouraging me. It was never to happen but it does happen these days with parents on the side lines showing an interest in what their sons were doing. I think maybe I was born to the world at the wrong time.

I believe I am looking for some form of closure. Once I am done with this I can get my memory block key and shut it forever.

As mentioned it has taken a while to write this book mainly because my hidden memories would reveal themselves now and again. I would shut them back in to my mental memory hidden box but wake up the next morning seeing that I had written my thoughts on a note book and would then read them. Not sure why but I stored all my notes and on taking the courage to read them all on the same day I decided my words needed to reach out to you.

All the times that I cried, I kept all things I knew inside, and it was hard but it was harder to ignore it.

CHAPTER FIVE- WORK HISTORY

The end of my school days were not easy, I had the intelligence to learn and study. Dealing with my earlier days made it difficult for me to revise for all of my final exams. I remember I did not revise and prepare myself very much. There were a few hours each week that I had a Human Biology class to attend that for obvious reasons I could not concentrate on some subjects. At this time I used to sneak out the school gates [wagging it] and sit in the local park gathering my thoughts then return for my next lesson on the agenda. Not sure how I got away with it as the teacher never reported it. In the examination room I remembered most things that my teachers had taught me. There were different exams every day over a period of a week depending on your chosen subjects. I was to get a high level pass GCSE in English literature, English Language, History, Sociology, Maths and Geography. It was obvious that my work career would involve using my mind and not my hands.

I left school with no real idea at what I wanted to do. Most kids these days have ambition of what they want to do after meetings with careers advisors; knowing what they are good at and seeking an apprenticeship in the now big wide world after school. For me I decided all I wanted to do was work and have the feeling of picking up my first wage packet. My independence was now all in my own hands. No more abuse, no more school and my life trail was all my own to follow wherever it would lead me to.

Within a few days I replied to an interview and got my first start. It was only as a shelf stacker in a supermarket, I was only fifteen at the time so it did not seem like such a bad idea. My first wage slip was twenty five pounds, not sure how that would compare to a living wage these days. It was enough for me as I had not discovered drinking and smoking at that time so I always had some left over at the end of the week. Still living at home with my mum and earning a wage; the done-thing then was to hand over some of your wage for your general upkeep and towards the bills.

I had been doing this work for a few years when I got called into the store manager's office. He said I did well at my job and had a lot of potential. He was now to promote me to the assistant store manager with a pay rise and even gave me a set of keys to open the store in the mornings. That was a lot of responsibility at my age but I was never late opening the doors, turning off the alarm and letting the staff in to prepare the store and work areas for the day ahead.

Now I was in a position of telling staff, rather than me asking staff what needed to be done as a priority each day. Some were a similar age to me and some a lot older that just needed some purpose and direction for the day. Eventually I got my own seat in the podium manager's office in the middle of the store. More amazing it was my responsibility to call head office once a week, each call lasted two hours, to place our weekly stock order based on what the store had sold the previous week and also looking for promotions for the week and where I would place it in the store. This was not an easy role because if you sold out of something a customer will go elsewhere to find it but also there was the risk of being over stocked on a product that customers were not buying.

Things changed. To my shock and surprise the store manager was doing his daily shop in our store at the end of the day and never paid for any of it. He was searched one evening while closing the door and was sacked. This was bad news for me as the new appointed store manager was a creepy guy and not very nice to me. Every day he wore the same old pin striped Navy suit and when talking to you and was constantly picking wax out of his ears. He said my ex-manager must have thought I was the best thing since sliced bread to open up the store in the morning while my manager had a lie in. He also drove an old sports car as a status symbol but as far as I knew he was way too ugly to have pulled a woman with him behind the wheel. Some people may say I am not with you for your looks but your personality, he had neither. I may sound a bit bitter but life has not treated me well so far. The next day I decided enough was enough and handed my keys in and walked out. At the time I was asked to stay over for an extra two hours with no pay, that was really taking me for granted so I did what I did with no regrets. In a way it would turn out to be like a godsend to me as at the time I was being considered for a transfer to manage one of their new stores .The responsibility and a career in retail, I am sure I could have climbed the ladder but I just had this gut feeling that I prefer being hands on and it would not have suited me.

A good friend of mine who is a qualified electrician took me on as his electrician's mate. It was mainly long hours in business properties so you could not dispute the daily running of the company premises, you were working but had access via a security guard. I learned a lot from it but the hours were not to my liking. Up on ladders and drilling cable runways and then pulling in the electric cables ready for termination was not really for me, I knew I was better than that.

While working as an electrician's mate I used to go to the trade counter at an electrical wholesalers to get bits and pieces for the job ahead. One day the manager served me due to being short staffed (that does not mean people working there were short and little.) He asked me why don't I come and work for him, I started the next day. I worked there for about a year before another opportunity came about. I got employed by another electrical wholesaler, which over the years was to become a major player in the infrastructure and networking industry. I ended up working for them for twenty-eight years in various roles including management and later on in international sales. I truly enjoyed my job to the extent that it was not just a job but my life. My long career there was to end and in further chapters I will refer to my time working there.

I was doing D.I.Y. at home and fell of a ladder and spent two days in hospital for observation due to having a punctured lung and two fractured ribs. On my discharge I spent a further day at home in bed relaxing. I really should have been off work for two to three weeks as advised by my doctor. Like a fool I returned to work after three days because I wanted to be there and not at home on my own in boredom. It turned out to be a bad decision; I was still in pain and should not have clocked in. We all make mistakes in our lives but this one caused me great pain and hurt mentally.

I was walking along the office and a member of staff was blocking my way to my desk, as he did most, days thinking he was cool walking around my desk talking to a customer on his hands free headset. I just felt at the time, we have our own desks and chairs and we all do company business from our own work station. In avoiding him I swore to myself under my breath due to a sharp pain in my fractured ribs. This was the event that was to end my career in a company that I had contributed so much. An obnoxious colleague with a chip on his shoulder that could have had an informal chat with me in a meeting room to solve the issue. Amazingly enough it was me that interviewed him and gave him employment. Not very liked within in the company he decided to go to Human Resources to say he had been swore at and threatened and in fear of his own safety. What an overstatement!

As with all incidents reported in the workplace they have to be investigated. While this was ongoing I was suspended and escorted off the premises, major shock and humiliation for a minor incident that could have been solved in minutes in a meeting room. Now it was time for HR to get witness statements from staff in the nearby area. Was I a criminal or just a dedicated employee whose only wish was to do his job to the best of my ability. It turned out that a lady who worked near me changed her statement from "I could not hear or see anything clearly as I was on the telephone." Later she would change her statement to back up the obnoxious twat to say she heard and saw it all. She was probably the worst person I had ever worked with, I could sense that she did not like me and would snap at me at times for no reason. Strange seeing that I spent so much of my time training her on products to do the job.

As there was now a witness, that would be the end of my days at a company that had been a pleasure and I was proud to work for. I got called in for a meeting to be given their decision and it was not a good one. I was not sacked but came to a compromise agreement for me to leave the company. I questioned managers and directors and they would just shrug their shoulders and say their hands are tied and it was all red tape. At the time I thought who the hell was running this company that clearly did want me to remain in the business. For the staff involved I really do wonder how they can sleep at night knowing that I could do serious harm to myself due to my known medical condition at the time.

False friends and colleagues are like our shadow, keeping close to us while we work in the sunshine, but leaving us the instant we cross into the shade.

The one day I was in a low mood and struggling to get myself motivated. The lady in question said to me "I am not your psychiatrist or psychologist so just get on with your job." That really hurt my feelings and maybe I should have reported it to HR. She even grabbed me by my arms the one day to let me know who was in charge. What if I had reported this? I chose not to.

All the words in my book ask the question, how do you explain it to people? The answer is you cannot. Best thing but maybe not the right thing is to alienate myself and pretend you do not want to know them. That way they do not have to deal with it or think they should help more. I would sooner be a recluse as everyone has busy lives and enough to deal with.

During my working week Monday to Friday in my long and satisfying career I got great satisfaction and focus for my mind, there was no time to think about anything else. But so be it that was yet another part of my life that was taken from me. This is not a sob story or a wish for you to feel sorry for me as it is only my words reaching out to you. Losing my career, I cannot let it break me down as I know that will result in total ruin for me. I really do not think I can win this battle of mind. Me versus Emotion, Reality and Truth.

The worse thing about it, on top of everything else, is knowing that I have let people down. That is hard to deal with as I was never really the type of person to put myself first, I am still not in my own strange way. I would like to think that in the last few years that I observe more and tend to find that I look for the mood swings of people and their bad days. Sometimes it can only take a few words and being honest with them to bring calmness.

You can bury a secret but you cannot bury the truth. Hate is a strange word that I never used but to loathe and dislike is acceptable to me, these people would be found out soon enough, I just wished it was today, they know who they are.

CHAPTER SIX- DEPRESSION

Now I will tell you about my depression years, suffering in silence. In the UK one in four of us will be affected at some point during our lifetimes but we still feel alone and people don't really understand that it is actually an illness. It is not easy to be open and honest for the fear of stigma and discrimination. It can affect anyone regardless of who you are or what you do. Attitudes regarding this subject may change if we are brave enough to open up and talk about it. It's like the worst flu all day and you can't kick it away. Feeling like the world has ended and that there is nothing positive to strive for anymore. I believe that one of the secrets of life is to have something to look forward to but I cannot find what I want and what I am supposed to be looking forward to. My state of mind at times is like telling myself, for me, for now, close the doors and shut the world away.

I can lose all sense of reality some days. I can have deep dark thoughts thinking there is no point to life because I am no good to myself or anyone else and the world, family and friends would have a better place without me. I have good and bad days but I never know which one it is going to be until I force myself out of bed in the mornings. Life just seems to be full of problems that I struggle to cope with and some days just burst into tears for no reason. Years and years of various medications were to follow.

I was always capable of doing my job as it was important to me to get a sense of achievement each day. There were many days when I would get home from work, turn the key in the door and be on a real downer. I would not cook or even switch on the TV. I would just sit alone in the dark with my thoughts. To make things worse apart from depression I ended up on further medication for anxiety and panic attacks. This confident and hard man was now becoming a wimp and a recluse.

How was I supposed to get my life back, get back on track? Even though I had my dark nights I could not find the answer or the light at the end of the tunnel, so to speak. Severe depression or bipolar can lead to many things, the worst being suicidal thoughts. It is estimated in the UK that over four thousand people a year commit suicide. I was to attempt it a few times but was never brave enough to see it through. I dread to think what is going through people's minds when they commit suicide. It even happens to rich famous people. The only reason I could not do it was out of love and respect for my family as my tragedy would also be theirs. It is sad that suicide and suicidal feelings are incredibly common. So why is it still such a taboo subject? Look out for the signs, talk about it with sensitivity and compassion. If even one person did that it would encourage us to seek help to end the stigma around the issue. We don't like to talk about it and can often not find the right words. Depression can also lead to mental illness that I will write about later.

Just think about it, every suicide is someone's child or friend. I am reaching out to you to get rid of this stigma and taboo as everyone deserves the chance to be happy again.

One in five people have dandruff; one in four people have mental health problems. I have both. As a person that has experienced episodes of depression, until I checked into a clinic, I did not realise how widespread mental health problems are. As mentioned, the trouble is nobody wants to talk about it and that makes everything worse. If you see it you need to remember who that person was and help them get back on to their feet and find themselves again. One of the most ignorant things is when you try to tell someone about your hurt and feelings, many people will change the subject without listening, that is something I was about to find out.

I once put a noose up in my garage out of curiosity to find out what it felt like around my neck but I could not go through with it thankfully. It would only take a few minutes and I could face the pain but not the pain I would leave behind me. I would rather see life each morning like it is a precious gift. If a car can be repaired back to a good condition, why can that not be done with a human being, in a lot of cases it is impossible and you are considered ready for the scrap heap.

Going back to an earlier chapter regarding my sexual abuse. His name was Jeffrey Davis and all I know is that he lived in the Erdington, Birmingham, area of the West Midlands. I was never invited to his house so that was also clever of him for obvious reasons. I would like to find out what happened to him but I doubt I will ever get that information back.

These days some macho car drivers hit the accelerator pedal heavy as if it was an extension of their own penis and manhood. Davis drove as if he had revised the Highway Code a hundred times. Thinking back now it would have been a risk to be to get pulled over by a police car for erratic driving. The question would be "Do you realise you were breaking the speed limit. Is that your son with you and why is he out so late when he has homework and school tomorrow" That would easily have caught him out as he suspected that I would say, no, he's not my dad. Therefore he was a careful driver and I think it was the only time I felt safe with him.

The visions that were planted in my brain were mine only. I suffered in silence, my memories not to be disturbed. Like a sign on the door of your hotel room. There were to be no cleaners allowed in that day as the only thing I needed cleaning was my thoughts and memories. That would not be part of the service, so not to be disturbed, go away, go away, it was one of my many bad days. If only I could I would have opened the door but felt it was to be of no avail.

I think I was locked in a thunder storm waiting for rain to

turn to sunshine. Don't believe it is something that will never be cured. It will lie dormant at times but I will always have it. You just have to learn how to deal with it. I slap my mask on, that mask is not just for other people you meet, it is for myself. It becomes a protective barrier, something I can use to convince myself I can get through whatever is thrown at me each day, a mask is like a false smile to me. The big fear was I am not sure if I was living my life the way I wanted to.

Speak out to whoever you feel able to, but most will not want to listen. Don't keep it in, do not ignore it. It does not help when I put my mask on when you feel you need to. When I am in a safe place I can sit silently or cry or open up to people or family that I feel comfortable with. It is now a better day, every day is different or unexpected. Then days are good as I wake up in the morning feeling not quite so bad.

Due to my mask not many friends or family could not see beyond the smile on my face and the hurt in my eyes. Real tears are useful for taking you to a place you want to go. You can be lonely in a packed room if the one person you want to be there is not there.

In my opinion male pride and depression are a deadly mix. Too often I refused that I needed help. I can bottle up my confusion until it overwhelms me. In my confusion I convince myself that a suicide attempt wouldn't destroy the family, they would be better off without me.

Depression now is more common and treatable and carries no shame, apart from the people who are ashamed of you and would rather turn a blind eye to the person they once knew but it is not the same person anymore. There are traumatic events in your life that can trigger it and I knew what my gun shot was. This has been a very hurtful experience for me that I have had to deal with. I feel like screaming out loud saying this is still me. Help me and don't run away because you do not understand it or admit it that it scares you.

Integrity, humanisation, degradation, euthanasia, ignorance is a virtue, manners are a must, treat people the way you want to be treated back, and one day life will bite you back, no hiding place, you will never get back what has been taken away from you. That is how I felt.

Heartache and promises and no shoulders to cry on. As the saying goes, if it is not broken then there is no need to fix it. But there comes a time when what is broken cannot be fixed, I guess that is me. The best medication from the beginning that I was subscribed was Diazepam. It is only allowed for two weeks because this drug is very addictive but eased the pain for me. Diazepam is actually used on the battlefield in wars when a soldier has been wounded, yes it is that strong.

I remember the one psychiatrist who had a small bed in her consulting room. She asked me to lie down on the bed and close my eyes and drift away to a time and place where I had felt comfortable and at ease. I did try but the only problem with that concept was that I could not remember or find this place that I was attempting to drift away to. She would calmly ask where I was now and what it felt like. I guess the answer she was looking for, was for me to reply that I was sitting on a beach somewhere, looking up at the clear blue sky without a care in the world. I can see the waves coming in from the seaside. My answer was, with no disrespect, that she was trying to help me. I said I am lying on this stupid bed of yours, feeling stupid, I did not drift anywhere or gain anything from it. I was never going to see her again. I did try but it was like studying a map looking for directions and on this map in my mind the place I was trying to visit did not exist or my mind refused to believe that it did.

CHAPTER SEVEN- SEEKING HELP

The stark truth is that a significant proportion of prisoners in our jails should not be in there at all. These unhappy men and women are not criminals in the common sense, but sufferers of mental illness. Instead of being subjected to the frightening thought of being locked in a cell they should be treated in hospitals or secure mental care homes. No one knows this better than me.

I once was having a really bad day and could not focus on anything, fighting a losing battle again. I managed to walk to my doctor's reception area and said I really need to see a GP. They could see I was in a bad state of mind with tears trickling down my face. I was told that unless I had an appointment I could not be seen that day. Stupidly I said OK I will just go home and kill myself. This must have worried them as I was picked up by a police car and put into a cell for the night. In fairness I was not seen as a criminal so my cell door was left open at night and in the morning with a police officer having to sit on a chair outside my cell totally bored and doing his best to stay awake.

I was seen as a danger to my own life. I should have been taken elsewhere but there were no available rooms or beds that could treat me and help me. Mental illness is not nice and has many different formats, you have no choice, I did not ask to be like this. Society and the government were not prepared for this so the one in four had nowhere to go, no facilities for treatment. In this now ever changing society who would give planning permission for a 'nuthouse' at the end of your nice safe road, it could take years. I was just crying out for help.

A worrying thing which I did once or twice was to have a tendency to imagine I was cured, of course on a rare good day. Then I would throw away my pills. This would cause a bad reaction as you cannot just stop taking prescribed medication. I had to be in control and reduce the strength or dosage to wean off them.

Women's jails are a particularly distressing example of these troubles. They hold less than five percent of the prison population, yet account for nearly half of the self-harm incidents.

Ideally, during a deprived and disturbed childhood, it is not right to be confined and sent to a place that could make your condition worse. Maybe it is improving now but back then you would just be someone who deserved further punishment and was not right in the head. It was understandable that they did not know any better, Taboo. Another failure of care in the community.

Some people suffer from Seasonal Adjustment Disorder (S.A.D), another illness that is not totally recognised. When the clocks change and daylight and night time change, when summer turns to winter, then some people go into their shell as if to hibernate like an animal. That did affect me but I already had the shell that is there for all seasons.

I wake most mornings after a dream or a bad dream and ask myself about the day before, confused and in some sort of mini trance before I am really functional or awake. I ask myself what was real regarding yesterday or what parts were a dream because my dreams seem real. As the day unfolds, questions to myself are answered, sometimes with relief, but tomorrow is another day.

Contrary to what most people believe 'Snapping out' of a true depression is impossible. The only way to escape its clutches is to do what I did, seek proper medical advice. As a general rule I often asked myself a lot of questions, mainly in the dark.

Did I have the following?

Tiredness and loss of energy;
Persistent low mood or sadness:
Loss of self-confidence and self-esteem;
Difficulty concentrating;
Feeling guilt ridden;
Avoiding other people;
Loss of appetite;
Loss of sex drive.

I ticked a yes to most of these so I seeked help, otherwise I would not be writing this book now.

Normal life + anxiety + major traumatic experience + Depression+ Mental health+ recovery. That may seem easy to explain but a lot of people never get over the finishing line to the recovery part. That is the best way I can explain it in my own words.

CHAPTER EIGHT- RELATIONSHIPS

I have always felt more comfortable in the company of women than other men. Maybe it felt like a safe zone due to my past. I did have very many good lads as friends and went on holidays abroad a few times a year for many years with them. Very good times as we all got on really well and had fun. These times are stored in my long term memory as happy days. I did not tell them about my childhood for fear of scaring them off and losing really good mates. Part of me did wonder how my sexual abuse would affect me in my teenage days and after; could I really hold down a loving relationship. I met my first real girlfriend who worked with me in my first job. In the canteen on lunch breaks she would smile and talk and she was so attractive and friendly, from then on I always looked forward to my lunch breaks. After that instead of sitting in a dull canteen we started to go outside for our lunch break and a lot of times we just talked and walked around the local music store.

   I really thought I had no chance with her but she saw in me qualities that I could not see in myself. We began dating and I was to end up with her for seven years. So at the age of eighteen to twenty-five I was not doing what most other lads my age were doing, I had found love and trust in her. It was about a year into our relationship that we both lost our virginity together. It was not the best as we were both nervous. She was golden and I do believe we could have spent the rest of our lives together and raised a family, it was not to be. Thinking back this was a nice time for both of us but maybe we met at a young age, confused where it was taking us, more confusion for me. It was a huge relief that I was experiencing sexual pleasure and not sexual abuse. Don't get me wrong, that was not the reason I was in a relationship. The mutual attraction and getting to know the person. Hearing about their family and childhood, although I did not reveal much of mine.

I do regret the way we ended, but I will never regret what we had, I was crying so hard when I got home. It was so unfair. I felt like we got that close that I was about to open my memory box to her. I still had my barriers around me so could not open up in case I was seen in another light and maybe with some disgust.

This was a pattern which was to repeat itself several times. I went out with girls and most times we would be together for a few years and become close to them. Sometimes the thought of it becoming more permanent or of the emotional connection strengthening I would break away. I just could not deal with it as I still had my demons inside my head. I am not proud of myself for this behaviour. I should not have got involved in relationships unless I was serious that my intentions were clear and I was prepared to open up and share everything together. I tried my utmost best but always failed at the final fence. As much as I tried I could not get over the final hurdle, I just kept falling back down and gave up.

I had always said to myself that I would never get married unless I met someone I truly loved and thought that it would last forever. If you find someone who makes you smile, who checks up on you often to see if you are okay, who watches out for you and wants the very best for you, don't let them go. Keep them close and don't take them for granted. People like that are hard to find.

My life was about to change for the better, at work we had a new accounts lady that I instantly liked. I liked her smile, her personality and she was very attractive but I just thought that she was out of my league. My same old thoughts were this could be hurtful for me, if I fall in love for the first time. Love can be different, there is loving someone or falling in love with someone, that is more intense and a true bond. I remember we had a works Christmas party for staff only and when I arrived and walked in the function room she was there and certainly stood out amongst the crowd.

I always did not like the fear of rejection and going back into my shell. I plucked up the courage to walk over to her, hello, how is your night so far. To my surprise she seemed pleased that I had come over the dance floor to talk to her. We ended up chatting for a few hours, sharing drinks and generally having a good time. This was my moment when the night was ending. I asked if she would like to go out for a meal sometime over our Christmas shut down break. She said yes and I was elated. There were other women there that night that I could have chatted up, but for me, once I meet someone I really like the others do not exist or are invisible.

Our first date went really well, a few drinks and a nice meal and we clicked perfectly and arranged to meet again. There was now a bounce in my step that I had never really felt before. Like the cat who got the cream, with a smile on my face. Driving to work in the mornings I played the same song each day on my CD player, titled The First Time Ever I Saw Your Face.

At the time I lived alone in my first home that I got a mortgage for. I was now on the property ladder feeling like the king of the castle, although it was not a castle but a basic two bedroom house. But it was my home and a new start. It felt great driving home from work and parking up outside my own house. Was I really finding my real self again, it felt like it and I started smiling again, being myself. The bad memories can stay locked away or even in the attic as far as I was concerned. Also at the time my partner had her own house in North Birmingham but I was in South Birmingham. She also had a six year old daughter from a previous relationship. I had always thought that I wanted kids of my own, to educate them, raise them with the right morals and basically ensure they did not have a childhood like mine. I adored my partner's daughter from the first time I met her. I would remain a part of her life until eventually she went away to university, I was very proud. We would do homework lessons together every evening when I got in from work, not always easy with a girl so young, there were many tears.

We had some great holidays together, the three of us, it was me finally dropping my barriers and the brick wall that was surrounding me. We had many good times and also bad times which I guess most families do. I got to the stage that I was spending most days at her house than mine. My house was sitting empty most of the time now. We decided it did not make sense financially and also we were a real proper couple now that should be sleeping under the same roof. After much thought and consideration I decided to move into my partners and daughters home. It was better that way as they could still be near to their family and friends and a very good local school.

Our relationship was solid, solid as a rock if you like. Before my house was sold we decided to stay at my house for the night. In advance I had purchased a bottle of Moet and Chan don champagne with the thought in my mind that I was going to ask her to marry me. I was a little bit anxious and nervous about what I was about to ask at it is not something you take lightly, it is a major change in your life that you have to be really sure about. I truly adored my stepdaughter and I still do. She has turned out well, intelligent and a good outlook on life in general. I did not get down on my knees as I felt that was too corny when I had seen people do it before. So I was sitting there with my thoughts and the words in my mouth, eventually I said will you marry me. She looked shocked and I thought she was about to choke on her champagne. Of course, when it is unexpected, some women cannot see sense and give you an answer there and then, understandably. She decided to have a think about it.

The next evening I was at her house not even mentioning the proposal, when she looked at me and said the answer is yes. This would lead to many months of planning. We decided to hire out a hotel resort for the day and have a civil wedding. It was an expensive day with one hundred sit down guests for the ceremony and meal and another one hundred guests for the evening reception and buffet. I will never forget it as it was one of the best days of my life. We remained married for many years and sold her house and purchased a nice big family home.

Things were about to change for the worse. We were sitting together one night watching TV when a programme came on about child sexual abuse. It was becoming more common now that people who had suffered in silence, like me, had decided to open up and report it. I could barely bring myself to watch this documentary. It was a memory that I locked away for a long time. I looked at her and said, "I am one of them, it happened to me." I told her more details and she was really shocked then angry about my family, who never reported it to the police due to the fact it could have prevented it happening to others. She was right but I was never sure if she looked at me the same way again. I had done it, I got my key and opened my mental memory box and turned it into a real memory.

It was not to be as simple as that though. My mind was now playing tricks with me, I could not focus and became very depressed. My head was spinning with my memories and viewing visions of what had taken place. I was feeling cheap and dirty and could not come to terms with these once hidden memories. I was running out of laughter to be replaced by sadness all over again.

So far I have had abuse and now the mental health problems were unexpectedly about to kick in.

CHAPTER NINE- A.P.E.

I will call this chapter A.P.E (acute psychotic episode.) I was now in a depressed very low mood after my revelation. I was in my house home alone. I had taken my various medications in the morning but could not remember if I had taken them, so on the afternoon I swallowed them again. Later on I had a rotten headache, maybe a migraine so I took two Nurofen tablets. Sat down and watched TV with a couple of cans of beer. What a mixture, what was I thinking of. The method in my madness was that I would sleep very well tonight and everything would go away, this was not to be.

I woke up during the night and opened my eyes to see a lot of bright lights shining on me. I know now that I was about to experience hallucinations.

Hallucinations are sensations that appear real but are created by your own mind. They can affect all five of your senses. For example, you might hear a voice in a room that no-one else in the room can hear or see an image that is not real. These symptoms can be caused by mental illness or the side effects of your medications.

What is happening now is worse than a nightmare. I was looking at both sides of my bed and there were a lot of little people standing there looking at me. I would hide under the duvet hoping that it was a bad dream and they would go away. I opened my eyes but they were still there walking around my bed. I looked to my left and on the bed there was a baby crying. I ran downstairs to the lounge and shut the door and curtains in the hope that it was just my bedroom that these, to me, real images were in. I turned off the lights and sat there in the dark confused and frightened. Then cats and dogs and various other animals started to appear, walking around my lounge.

I went and shut myself in the conservatory but there were

strange people in the garden trying to get in and staring at me through the glass windows. I made my way back upstairs to sleep in the spare room and shut the door and close my eyes thinking that this will all go away tomorrow. It was not to be as the little people were now walking out of my wardrobe to gather around my bed. Still, after all these hours it all seemed very real to me. It was about to get worse. At times when I dozed off for a while due to tiredness I would be woken by voices coming from inside my pillow. I pulled my pillow apart to see where the voice box was buried but there was nothing in the pillow.

The next day seemed to be a bit of a relief for me, daylight shining through the window and no little people or animals in sight. The voices returned again but this time as if they were from speakers hidden in the walls. I answered back to them, talked to them. It was now that my wife and stepdaughter were showing concern for me. It was all real to me but not then to the extent I thought they were part of the conspiracy. My mobile phone was switched off but I still picked it up as a voice was talking to me on it. I had a pair of shorts on and started talking to the buttons on them as another form of communication. I then thought what are all these people doing in my house, it must be rigged with microphones and cameras as no matter what room I would walk in, the voices would say "You are in the kitchen now and I like what you are wearing today."

I thought there must be some central point in my house, like a network, that this was all coming from. I went up into the loft and searched everywhere trying to find it. This behaviour had gone on for a few days now so my wife booked me a doctor's appointment which I was reluctant to go to. On arriving we sat at reception but then I started to talk to my pen as if my voices had followed me here. I went outside and stamped on my pen until it was in little pieces. Sitting back down in the doctor's reception area I started to talk to my trainers. God knows what the other people in the waiting room must be thinking. My name got called out for my appointment and I took my trainers off and left them outside hoping for no more voices in the doctor's surgery.

That did not work as the voices always found a way to get inside my head. I remember my doctor looking a bit surprised with my behaviour as if he had never seen anything like it before. This situation was way above his qualifications so my wife was given an emergency phone number to get me a home visit from professional people that had dealt with this kind of illness before. This was arranged for the following day as although I was off my head I was not a threat to anybody.

That night I went to bed with my wife but could not sleep in the main bedroom where it all started. Tonight it was going to be the spare bedroom even though I knew the little people would be in there somewhere. We lay down to go to sleep, I held her so tight as a kind of security blanket, hoping my demons would leave me alone tonight.

I was to wake up during the night, when she was soundly asleep; the voices were talking to me again. They were telling me to meet them at the bottom of my road on the corner. I got out of bed and walked down the stairs, opened the front door not realising I had left it wide open. Now I was walking the streets barefooted, talking to these voices to direct me where they are. If the voices had told me to stand in the middle of the duel carriageway I am certain that I would have done. I must have been there for an hour shouting "Where are you."

My wife must have woken up and turned over to notice that I was not there. She walked down the stairs to look for me only to see that there was no sign of me and the front door was left open. In panic she walked around the block trying to find me. She walked back home, not really knowing what to do next so she called the police, explained the situation and would they go out and find me. It must have been another hour later when a police car pulled up next to me with my wife inside. They explained calmly that they just wanted to get me back home safely. They even came inside our house and had a cup of tea to try to talk to me and understand what state of mind I was in.

A few hours later I had my home emergency visit but I did not really speak to them as I was too busy talking to the voices inside my head. They had made their decision that I was to be taken to a mental health hospital to talk with a number of consultants. I refused, I have always been strong willed and if I make a decision I would stick to it unless I was proved wrong. That same morning my sisters and brother arrived at my house due to a desperate phone call from my wife, bless her. I could tell they were shocked with what I was going through. I was always close to my sisters so when they persuaded me to go to this hospital, I said yes OK then.

This was to be another experience as the voices came along with me for the journey. I was sitting in a room with a few doctors and some students that were learning and starting their career. I was very nervous and panicky being surrounded by so many people. A few times while in there I would hear an announcement over the tannoy saying there was a telephone call for me. I was later to find out that there was no tannoy system ever installed in that hospital.

So that was that for me, I was told that I was being admitted to their mental health ward for tests, new meds and rehab. I did not have any choice in the matter, it was either say yes voluntarily and be cared for but if you said no then you would be sectioned under the mental health act with less privileges. I said yes ok and was led to what was to be my home for a short while. Well at least I thought so but I ended up being in there for three months as I was in such a bad state of mind.

If you know the person I was you would be very surprised and shocked. Most people that found out where I was did not visit me as I guess they did not know what to say to me. I was now in the system but did not realise at the time, once you are in it, it is difficult to get out of it and it would take many years.

If my childhood days were different I would not be in this state now. I guessed it would catch up with me one day in my adult life but never imagined that it would lead me into the doors of a mental hospital. As I mentioned earlier I am now a number on a list in a system that tries to care. I had eventually, but through choice, made it into the one in four, how unlucky of me to be one of that number. A statistical reminder of a world that doesn't care.

I can understand why some people might look at me and say "What has he got to be depressed about?" I got that a lot, where mental health issues seem to be a big taboo. Only trust someone that can see in you, the sorrow behind your smile, the love behind your anger, and the reason behind your silence.

CHAPTER TEN- MENTAL HEALTH HOSPITAL

See this is it, I am about to start on my next journey, not sure where it is going to take me. Maybe to that light at the end of the tunnel. I was now officially an inpatient to what I will refer to as Hope Springs. My hospital and new home.

I now have my own private room, well kind of private as I was not allowed to lock my door for obvious reasons. Staff would walk in every hour to check that I was OK. Even during the night they would continue to do this, but this time with a torch shining on me. My room consisted of a single bed, a wardrobe, a chest of draws and a sink. It also had a window with a view of a brick wall and also with metal bars on it. There would be no escape from here. Welcome to my new home.

My first few days in this hospital I have no memory of due to being drugged up on medication, so what I will write to start with my time in here is what I was told from my family members on their visits.

In the beginning, hospital for me was a strange place that I initially thought, why am I in here. I was about to realise this was the place that was going to let me find myself again. On strong medication my demons were batted away and out of reach and would not trouble me or find me here, I was safe, sound and secure with no need to hide under my duvet anymore.

I was allocated my new medication on my first day here, I will call them smarties. Then I was put to bed to let my body and mind adjust. My wife and sister were to visit that evening after going to a supermarket to get me some essentials. Pyjamas, robe, slippers and some other bits and pieces. I was later told that they were crying while walking around the shop while buying these items for me. There are set hours for visiting and also visitors are not allowed in a patient's bedroom. As it was my first day in here an exception was made and they both were allowed to go to my room to give me my various items.

I was totally out of it to the extent that I did not recognise my own wife and sister. I was saying "Who are you?" which resulted in further tears. They thought I was here short term until a doctor told them on leaving that I was going to be here for a few months. I did not know that at the time. It was like I was in hibernation, knowing that when I wake, my memories could return at any time.

That was my worry and until this day it still is. It is a feeling that is difficult to describe. Some days I will wake up feeling good and ready for the day ahead but some days I would with unexpected bruises on my arms and legs. This would be the result of a bad nightmare when I punched and kicked out during the night. One of my worst dreams was being on a football pitch with the football in front of me waiting to score a goal. I kicked and kicked and tried to kick the ball but I could never reach it, maybe that is where some of my bruises came from during the night. On days like that I felt like I was blindfolded and tossed into a day that I did not want to be in. These days were the bad days or even dark days. Curtains closed, in the dark and hoping tomorrow would be a good day.

Some days it was peaceful but other days, it was like a torrential storm with hailstones bouncing off my mind. In situations like that it was not for me to scream help, help, but wait it out for the calm after the storm.

On my first day in Hope Springs I did not behave very well as my A.P.E. was still in my mind. My first day was also not my best, so I was told. In the large open ward seating area I was climbing on tables trying to remove light fittings as I thought that the voices were in them and following me. I tried to remove the smoke alarms as I thought there was a camera in them watching me. Then I went to the toilet and tried to escape out of this small window. But in doing that it set of an alarm to the staff on their key ring buzzers. I was sedated again and put to bed.

We all had a label that nursing and security staff were aware of. Each morning they would have a meeting before breakfast to discuss the previous day and the day ahead.

Grade 1 Patient: Cannot leave the ward, not allowed in the garden without a member of staff to stand next to you and watch you.

Grade 2 Patient: Allowed to leave the ward and sit in the canteen or garden unattended.

Grade 3 Patient: the above plus the luxury of asking for one hour pass out to leave the hospital unattended to go to the local shop and newsagents.

It had taken me a month to get to grade three patient grade. A luxury and a sense of pleasure in feeling free for an hour. Deep breath and sucking in the air like it was you last breath of freedom even though I was walking to the corner shop in my slippers. I had to sign in and out noting the time of the day. If you were late back your pass would be taken away from you. It was known that some patients had not returned for a day or two but would be eventually be found and seen as a risk. This meant their hospital stay would be extended. Once caught, they were put in the sectioned ward while under the influence of drugs or alcohol. To me, it was just not worth trying to attempt that, I was feeling safe so why would I want to run away. They knew it was a temptation as the local corner shop also sold beer. But although I felt 'oh why not', the feeling of self-control triumphed, so that my meds would continue working for me. Signing back in on time made me feel like a responsible person again.

That little time and sense of freedom, walking without

slippers on sometimes, looking up at the clear blue sky, drifts away for the moment. It wakes you up to the fact of how much we take for granted. When you get that wakeup call then it is time to revaluate your life. I was there for rehab, it was best to sit it out, accept the care and treatment I was getting. The staff seemed to like me as a person and not a number that meant nothing to them. Their goal was the same as mine, the road to recovery.

There was a nurse's room in my open ward stocked with all the smarties to treat us. Depending on your original assessment each patient had a file that was with the nurse so she could ensure that she was giving me the right meds. I had to take them in front of her in case a patient decided not to swallow them. Med times were three times a day, morning afternoon and night. My name would be called out by the nurse to come in and take my meds, then she would tick in my file. At the night call you had the option of a sleeping tablet, some nights I accepted if I had a really bad day.

There were care workers on the ward at all times of the day, male and female. There was a staff rota board on the wall that is updated every morning. I smile when I see certain members of staff were to be on duty that day. The ones that seem to really care, make the effort to sit down with me in the open ward area, share a coffee with you, talk about how I was feeling. Sometimes they would sit down with me for a while and play a game of chess or scrabble with me. I had total respect for them and I guess they could sense that as there were some unruly patients on the ward that caused them grief.

Meal times were always nice, the nurse must have given me a smartie to increase my appetite. I must have looked frail because on my first day I was only nine stone and six pounds in weight, on my release or discharge I had gained almost two stone in weight. The food was to a very good standard with a few choices. Each morning at breakfast I was given what I will call a small menu from which you chose what was to be your choice for the next day's meal. There would be three choices for my starter, main meal and dessert. Most weeks options were varied each day. Meal times would be 8am breakfast, 1pm lunch, 5pm evening meal and the 10pm for cocoa and biscuits before bedtime. It was all really nice now I was being looked after properly compared to my childhood days.

To a little surprise for me there were two Asian men on my ward. Based on their religion, there are some food items they would not eat. It proves that no matter what race or walk of life you are from, if you have a brain that is not functioning properly then it could happen to anyone.

My first few days at Hope Springs, I walked around like a zombie with pyjamas and slippers on, all day long. Out of my bedroom window I could see birds flying away with their freedom. At the time I wished I could fly with them, never to return again. For me, escape was not a possibility, although I did try a few half-hearted suicide attempts, a cry for help that really did not reach out to the people that I wanted to see my tears.

The mornings were becoming my favourite part of the day after the eight hours at night and morning when you are not allowed to leave your room to sit in the open ward. As early as 7am the coffee trolley would be wheeled out to get your caffeine fix for the morning ahead. I would take two cups of coffee with me outside and sit on a bench in the garden, mostly on my own and light up a cigarette while waiting for the breakfast to come out. After that it would be newspaper and book times.

Each morning some of us would give a list to a patient who had an hour pass to go to the local shop. The one patient in particular would ask if we needed anything from the shop, collected our money and kindly returned with our items, he was clearly on the mend and waiting for his discharge letter. After one month, once I had gained the trust to get my pass out, I would be doing the same for other patients. Sometimes a queue was waiting for me after breakfast. I liked doing that for them, a little bit of responsibility for me, even though it was only coming back with a full carrier bag from the shop. One thing I refused to get from the shop was booze, I will explain this later on.

There were a few cases, more seriously troubled on my ward. Now and again a patient from the sectioned area in another part of the building would be transferred to a room on my ward. Either for good behaviour or maybe they had just blagged it and fooled the care workers. This type of patient would rarely have a visitor, maybe they were disowned by family due to their behaviour and mental health problems and they would rather not face it or try to deal with it. Every person was someone's son, it was wrong.

This type of patient would not have any spare cash in their pocket. I had to wise up to this as they would be taking cigarettes and even cash from more vulnerable patients. I felt really sorry for them when I saw it happen. I would make it clear when they approached me that they would get nothing from me. I pretended to seem like to them that I was not the kind of man to give in and they would regret if they messed with me. It worked and I was getting stronger in body and mind.

Visiting times were a part of the day that I looked forward to. I would have two hours after lunch and two hours on the evening. I did not always get a visitor during the day due to their commitments that for me was understandable.

My main visitor was my wife, which I will always be thankful for. She had a full time job, a daughter to spend time with and a husband in a mental health hospital. How she coped I really do not know but she was always there for me when I needed her, putting her own needs to one side for another day.

She was wonderful and amazing, bringing me clean

clothes and taking home my dirty washing, also a bag of goodies for my room. Most of my family would also visit me a few times during the week. I was one of the lucky ones that had people who cared for me, some did not. You can choose your friends but not your family. I was proud of both.

Regarding visitors I had decided that I did not want good friends and work colleagues to visit me. It would be difficult for both of us to understand how a healthy, intelligent, respected man had ended up in a place like this. It would have been too awkward a moment with them on edge, not really knowing what to say to me, Taboo.

There was one of my family that did not visit. She imagined my new home was going to be like the classic film *One Flew Over the Cuckoo's Nest* starring Jack Nicholson. It was nothing as bad as that, well most days anyway.

I was one of those people who put too much emphasis on work my and career and it took its toll on my relationships, physical health, my emotions.

The further I look and think back, the more I discover. How many of us can look back, I wonder, and can recall that childhood moment when we were so happy. An innocent child with the future in their hands with no idea how ugly the adult world can be.

CHAPTER ELEVEN- LIFE IN HOSPITAL

That is it for now about my new home, meals and visitors. Now I will take you to entertainment times and other patients. There was also a weekly board placed in my ward listing various things to pass the day away. It was good to keep patients minds active and not be sitting there all day staring at the walls and for them to start feeling sorry for themselves. It was no holiday camp but the list of things we could put our names down for were:-

Daytime Bingo

Evening quiz time

Some time in the gym (providing you had a certificate for fitness)

Pool tournament

Table Tennis tournament

Relaxation therapy

Do some gardening

Go to a drawing and painting class

Watch the daily movie in the cinema room

All of these had a calming influence on patients and also to form a trust with other patients. You would be surprised that some patients that seemed to be reclusive would open up. Also some patients that were over active would withdraw so we were all on the same level, just for a while at least.

There was to be further entertainment on the ward some days but this time from other patients. On my ward today was this man, I did not know his name as he was too far gone to try and talk to him. He was sitting on his own and started shouting out, "I didn't shoot John Wayne, it wasn't me." This would continue for most of the afternoon. It is not a good idea to start laughing at another patient having a bad day but it did make me smirk. It was to be not a good choice but today's movie in our mini cinema was *True Grit* featuring John

Wayne. Now the shouts were "he is alive, I can see him, I did not shoot him."

Another day there was another grown man who came out of his room with a pair of socks on his hands and on his feet. He got down on all fours and starting crawling around the ward barking at us as if he was a dog for the day. It was very sad but no one laughed. I did try to calm him down, stroked his back and said, "It is OK, it is OK, I will go and get you a dog biscuit." I was not very proud of myself for saying that to him.

Another day a woman patient walks in from the garden area into our men's ward. She was quite attractive. Then she started shouting "Who wants me, who wants me, you can take me anyway you want." Of course there were no takers and she was soon restrained and put back on her ward, with a jab I guess. I did not see her in the garden area for a few days. One day she walked into the garden with a member of staff to watch over her. She sat next to me on my bench and she had bandages on both wrists. At dinner time she had picked up the knife and slashed both of her wrists. She confided in me that she had been raped, not once but twice. Not only will the scars on her wrists remain forever but also the scars in her mind that will never go away.

Today the sun is shining, clear blue sky and a nice relaxed atmosphere. A lot of patients have decided to sit out on the benches in our shared garden area. I managed to get my usual bench at the top of the garden in the corner. I would sit on my own most days, still a little confused as to why I was in here. This afternoon in the garden we were about to see some unwanted entertainment, especially the lady patients.

Two days previous a man, short and fat, was moved from the section ward into my ward. A nurse told me it was because he needed to interact with other people to try and get him out of his shell that he had created for himself. For those two days he just walked up and down the ward in his Aston

Villa shirt and shorts. Today for the first time he was allowed out in the garden. What he did next was very funny to me at the time but maybe not for others. While in the garden he took of all his clothes and run around the garden as naked as the day he was born, his birthday suit. He was running around with his penis in his hand and shouting, "Come play with this, feel it, does anyone want it." He got restrained and put back on the sectioned ward, some women were really upset that day, and after all they were very delicate and scared. Not your ideal full Monty.

Today we had a new patient admitted on to my ward. Tall, medium build, he seemed really spaced out and doped up. Every day, for the first week he would walk and pace around with the same pyjamas on. After this I was sitting on my bench in the garden when he started to walk towards me, this time wearing jeans and a T-shirt. He seemed relaxed and sat down next to me and asked for a cigarette, I handed one to him and lit it up. Then he would stand up and walk around the perimeter of the garden, in a trance, I guess he had a lot on his mind the he was trying to break down and digest his thoughts. Problem was he came back four more times asking for another one, I obliged but by now I was fed up with it and told him he would not get any more, he then walked away. He returned later and handed me fifty pounds and asked me, each day when I go to the shop can I buy him twenty smokes and in return also buy twenty smokes for myself, a good deal for me, so I thought at the time. In a place like this you need to be careful that you do not get over friendly with another patient. It's maybe good to have a pal that you can share your thoughts and feelings with, vice versa, while we see out our time in here but it's not a good idea.

There is still a lot that I am angry about but I choose what I can fight against and what I cannot. It is fight or flight. The sense of any danger to you, can either fight or run away from it. To me this was a situation that would still be there in the morning.

One evening, my stalker approached me and told me that my room was opposite to his. I said I did not know that as I tend to keep myself to myself. He then said "Tonight do you want to sleep in my bed with me or shall we sleep in your bed. My blood began to boil and my temper got the better of me. As mentioned earlier, one of the reasons I ended up in here was due to my memory being released. This was not a moment I wanted or was proud of. Part of my features is that I have big hands that seem out of place with my arms. My instant reaction was to grab him by the throat, pin him up against a wall, I made it as clear as day that I was not a homosexual, I am disgusted, never come near me again. I went and sat down with my head between my legs and my hands over my ears, I was in a state of shock. Sitting on the ward that night there were three care workers sitting at the same table having a general chat and observing the activity on the ward. I knew I could now look after myself but felt a bit vulnerable. I walked over, pulled over a chair and explained my situation. I could tell by the expression on their faces and the changing look in their eyes that they were now concerned about me.

For the next two nights they would take it in turns to sit outside my room door, they must have been really tired and bored. The reason for this is because patients are not allowed to lock their room doors so this was a way to protect me while I got some sleep, not that I really managed a few hours those nights. It was a busy ward so when a patient was discharged, they moved him into a room nowhere near me. I felt safe again now, protected, it is hard to say but it felt like home. It was my hiding place.

The next day I got my big bottle of Lucozade, a good book and some snacks and sat on my bench in the garden. I could not believe it, this man that I had told never to come near me again and was told by the care workers to just leave me alone. He decided to sit next to me on the bench. I asked him to find somewhere else to sit but he refused. I asked him to stand up and discuss this, which he did. I am not proud of it but after a few heavy punches I had decked him. The ladies in the garden all ran inside thinking I was a nutter on the loose and reported it to security staff. If only I was older and wiser enough I would have done that to Davis.

I was restrained and taken to the front meeting office with security and care workers sitting down at the table with me. I was shaking and dreading that they would put me on the section ward. Once the care workers explained the reason for my behaviour they agreed that I could stay on my ward but downgraded to a level two patient. I could sense that my every movement was being watched. Obviously any form of violence within the hospital was not to be tolerated. I was a friendly patient who followed the rules but the circumstances for me just caused me to snap. I also put my foot firmly on his foot, no chance of kicking out from him. I was nearly about to do a solar plexus on him – this is a hard hit with your palm to the lower chest that disables them for a few minutes, dulls the nerves and allows you to walk away – but decided to let the staff deal with it.

At evening visiting time tonight, we could sit on the ward or if it was nice, sit with them in the garden. I could not work out why this group of patients and visitors would all sit together most evenings at the top of the garden. I found out the reason why when I was asked to join them. Their visitors were coming in with plastic bottles of coca cola and lemonade. What was inside the bottles was alcohol, vodka amongst others. That was why they were out there minds on a high. Feeling like they were back in the real world and booze would numb their reason for being here, until the following morning when you wake up with a hangover and reality bites again.

I never did join in with that group of patients, I just could not see or understand it. The reason I was in here was to be treated and well enough to eventually go home, getting drunk at night in the garden would be defeating the purpose of me being here. Most patients smoked in here, maybe some of them had never had a cigarette in their life until they landed in here. Counterfeit cigarettes are readily available on the ward if you have the right contacts that can trust you. The main one being Jin Ling, originally from China but now produced in Russia. On tests, I once read a report, that they contained industrial chemicals and asbestos. At two pounds a packet, even though they tasted like camel shite, they served the purpose of passing time away and thinking time. Each weekend a man with a carrier bag full of Jin Ling would enter our ward signed in as a visitor and hand over the bag to his contact in return for cash. The contact would hand them to patients in a private area. I am not sure if staff were aware of it, maybe they were and just turned a blind eye, if the patients are calmer then their job would be easier.

CHAPTER TWELVE- HEALTH REVIEWS

I have been a patient for a month now. The next procedure every two weeks is to have a patient review. This would normally be with the nurse in charge of my ward, the doctor / consultant and a member of my family. It would be an assessment of my medication, my behaviour on the ward based on feedback from staff. It feels like a parole board for a prisoner hoping to be released out on bail or in my case, as an outpatient due to good behaviour and signs that my recovery is working well. Released to the outside world with no threat to society. There was a meeting room in the middle of my Waiting outside the door it felt like sitting in a doctor's surgery waiting for your name to be announced, "Thomas Piggott, room number two please."

It was obvious to the other patients on the ward, a few were also about to have their reviews, the reason for being called into the room. There would be the odd comment from another patient to say good luck, you can do it, stay calm and relax. I would say that some patients were hoping for the good news that they were being discharged, to be with their family. In a sad way some patients were hoping that they had failed the review so that they could wait another two weeks for the next one. It was a comfort zone so some felt they were not ready to be released to the outside world, maybe because their home life was not very good. There were also some patients that could not be discharged as they had no home to go to for various reasons, like some families did not want them back home. For these ones they were put on a waiting list for a secure care home as there was nothing else that this hospital could do for them. And also they needed the bed for a new patient, swings and roundabouts I will call it.

My review went OK I suppose but it was decided I should still remain in here for a while longer. Some patients would come out of the room crying, I just accepted it, there was no appeal process anyway, so what will be will be.

There are to be some sad stories of patients who were discharged but could not cope without the care and attention that was provided here.

Institutionalized not only happens in prisons but also on mental health wards. Once you have been deprived of independence and responsibility. When you are returned to the ward, after a long time, some cannot cope with the demands of life in general. They would commit suicide or deliberately do something wrong so they could be re-admitted.

I will explain one instance of this, for a man that would sit next to me on our ward during meal times. I was one of the few that talked to him and to an extent looked out for him. After his review he was given the news that after three months in here, he was to be given an all day and overnight pass to return to his flat. I could sense it was not a good idea, I was proved to be right. On walking out of the ward and passing through security and reception he handed in his pass out document and then the doors were opened for him. I know what happened next, because he told me on his return. He lasted only a few hours in his flat, staring at four walls wondering if where he was sat now was his real home.

He went out to the chemist and purchased a mixture of pain killers and headache tablets. He had done a suicidal overdose, luckily a neighbour on hearing that he was at home decided to knock on his door to say hello. He did not answer so she tried the door and found that it was not locked. She found him lying on the floor with lots of pills next to him. An ambulance was called and he was taken to the Manor hospital and had his stomach pumped. After two days he was returned to Hope Springs and I sensed a slight smile on his face.

This evening a patient fell asleep in his room and was too late to get his meal. The food had all been eaten. He was hungry and angry so he tried to knock the kitchen door down so that he could search the fridge and cupboards looking for something to eat. The staff warning bleep was alerted and activated. He also ended upstairs on the section ward and he was given some food through a hatch on his new room door. How many patients are up there I do not know. I just sat there in the corner of the ward reading a book. That is why other patients would nickname me "The Professor" because I was always reading and writing notes about my time in here.

Later on during the night while we were all sitting on our ward. Some were reading, some were watching TV, arguing over the remote control, and some just pacing up and down the ward waiting for cocoa and biscuit time. It was odd for a new patient to be admitted at night time, he was escorted in, a bit drunk and doped up and allocated a room. He came and sat on the ward before lights out, he was still on a high and outspoken. The fool, who obviously did not realise what he was doing or even where he was, took a wad of cash out of his pocket and spoke out, "How do I spend this while I am in here." When it was time for bed and lights out we all went to our rooms. As soon as his head would hit the pillow he would be out of it and ready to snore.

Breakfast time the next morning he came running on to the ward, telling staff his money was stolen during the night. Easily done as you were not allowed to lock your bedroom door, also due to his brash attitude he had left himself open to that possibility. The person who did this terrible thing to a fellow in patient was never found out, never mind the cash. I had been on the ward by now for a long time and in my mind I have a good idea of who would have quietly sneaked into his room that night but decided to keep my mouth shut, I had no proof, also it could have caused me to be in danger.

I think to me it was obvious who it was because he escaped the next day. There was no easy way to get out of here but he managed to crawl up a wastepipe, get onto the roof in the garden, then jump down and out and he was now on the run to spend the money that he had robbed. It was two days before he was caught and found, that resulted in him spending an entire month locked up on the section ward. I later found out that he was due to be discharged in a week so it was a really silly and off the head thing for him to do. Who knows what goes on in people's heads in here, I only know mine.

Today was my next patient review which also reminds that I have been in here for two months. Earlier in the week I had further blood tests done so this was not only about a discharge date, but also some good or bad news. I was told that I would remain in here for another two weeks but that was not the end of my assessment though, as there was more information to follow, regarding my blood test results. I was told that I had a 50 / 50 % chance of developing "Korsakoff's Syndrome." It was explained to me that this syndrome is a brain disorder. There are many reasons that it can develop, including a traumatic experience in your life that you have never really coped with, not taking your medications as instructed, or even having a binge drink on a bad day to make things go away. Over the years it would catch up on you.

It is not strictly speaking a form of dementia but it means at times I will experience less of short-term memory. This syndrome is likely to develop gradually. If it is suspected, as it was with me, immediate treatment is essential.

I was to have a nurse visit my room each day for two weeks. This would involve me dropping my pants and lying face down on my bed. Then the big syringe and needle would be slowly inserted into a vein on my backside, ouch. All this treatment was done to reverse the symptoms at an early stage, it is known as a B12 injection. Lucky me, or not, but to this day it has not developed any further. But there were other patients on my ward who were worse off than me and did not respond too well to their treatment. I just went outside and sat in the garden on my own, with my thoughts, until darkness.

The following day was to be a very sad day. There was a lot of trauma and screaming on the ward. I was told that a young Asian lad had managed to hang himself in the lift. I remember trying to speak to him that day as he seemed troubled and confused with his new surroundings. It was all too hard to take in and digest, he had his reasons for this tragedy that I will never know, but in a way I understood as I had been close to it myself.

To run away from trouble is a form of cowardice, while it is true that the suicide braves death, he does it for some noble reason or object to escape some ill that he cannot deal with anymore. One of my favourite movies is *It's a Wonderful Life*. It is about a man who wants to commit suicide and is presented with reasons not to. If only he had watched it.

Everyone is sometimes sad, but what if someone close to you seems to be sad for a longer time. It will be like me losing interest in things I had previously enjoyed. It could be hobbies, spending time with family and friends, sport, and even sex. Loss of appetite, losing weight. Uncontrollable emotions, mood swings.

I am not feeling sorry for myself and it does not define me as a person. It is not a choice, it is a complex mental disorder. It is like there is a cloud following me around and I cannot make it stop. I take medication to balance the chemicals in my brain. I am trying my hardest as I do not want to feel ashamed for my depression. I am a real person, I am not broken, and I take responsibility for myself just as any other person.

Another new day for me, like a groundhog day. Patients in here do not care about personal hygiene, for me it was a must to feel clean and refreshed for the day. I would go to my room after breakfast to pick my toiletry bag then go into the ward cupboard to collect a clean towel.

Each patient was monitored each day by the staff on duty.

One member of staff's role for the day would to have a list of patients on my ward. Every hour she would walk around the ward, the gardens, canteen, rooms, even the patient pass out book. Every hour it would be her job to tick all the boxes so all the patients were accounted for.

I did not like my shower mornings, you could close the door but it was not a shower cubicle. An open space with a tiled floor with a shower head on the ceiling. Just to rule out self-harm there was a round window on the door for all to look in and see. I suspected that a male member of staff was gay, the way he walked and talked, for a man, did not seem right. At my shower time on some days he would be staring through the window until I turned the shower off and wrapped a towel around me. Due to my experience after showers on my football days, it made me feel very uncomfortable and ashamed.

While watching television on our ward, some patients believed that the people on the screen were talking directly to them. Could be risky if it was an action movie. You will find that the vast majority of people who have a form of mental illness will never hurt anybody.

Tomorrow was to be my next review so I sat in my room alone just thinking about it. On this review it was decided that I could have a weekend pass out. Saturday morning until Sunday evening, in the care of my wife. It felt good that moment I walked through the front door of my real home. I suppose you could say home is where the heart is. I thought my dog was going to pass out, my best friend, he was so pleased to see me again.

Saying "Hello fat boy," to some people would be an insult but as I had never had it said to me before it felt good. I laughed for the first time in a long while. We all settled down, talked and had a nice meal together. Now I was in relaxed mode so I decided to have my first can of beer in ten weeks. It tasted horrible but good, it's a man's thing. I once worked with a guy who said he does not like beer, how strange, but it was a laugh moment that I guess he wished he had not revealed to us.

At bed time I was very anxious and a little part of me was having a panic attack, which I did my best to conceal. I would be sleeping in the bedroom where I first saw my little imaginary friends and animals. I rested my head on the pillow and pulled the quilt over my head. I was afraid to close my eyes, now and then I would take a peak around the room to see if my imaginary friends had come back to taunt me again. I did not sleep very well that night but I was relieved to have got through the night with no demons or thoughts coming after me again.

Unlike Hope Springs, where I felt safe and secure, in the daft thought they would not be able to find me in here. This may seem wrong, but for now, I was looking forward to returning to Hope Springs. It was a new way of life for me. I knew that on my return there would be a review about how I coped outside the walls and there was a very good chance I would be discharged as an inpatient to an outpatient. I needed to be ready for this and to brave up, to get back to reality, society and work.

CHAPTER THIRTEEN- THE MIND OF AN ABUSER

I have been trying to understand the mind of a child abuser. I have done a lot of research in books, library and on the internet. Mostly what I will now write is based on my own personal opinions and views.

In his earlier life he must have been a decent law abiding citizen. What reason could have changed him into a child predator?

Listening to my secrets, listening to an unstable boy, there must have been a gleam in his eyes. He would then spend time with me and provide me with all I needed, like a vulture, he knew I had no father figure. Most children want to talk about themselves, school, friends, and homework and want their parents to seem interested. Even as an adult I would come home from work hoping anyone would ask me how my day had been, basic nice interaction.

A boy like me felt like no-one was listening to them. I would tell him some private information and so would he, with the promise of me not telling my mom or family. Then he would visit my home to talk to my mom knowing that tonight his luck was to begin again. He was clever and mentioned the odd casual question, as a test to see if I had spoken out. I had not so then he knew he had this boy's trust. This is when in his mind he would think, "He is mine now, I can do what I want with this boy."

In the abusers childhood days maybe he was bullied, picked on at school, isolated, and a chance he was sexually abused. Maybe he thought this way was normal and he had lost all sense of dignity. For me it was the opposite. I would never harm a child in my life, never have, and never will. I could never put a child through what I went through. The feelings of self-shame, a burden to carry all your life, the feeling of having to shower all the time as you feel unclean. I still think back now, talking to myself, saying "why was I so naïve to be captured like that? Then I cry and telling myself "You were only a child Tommy, not even a teenager yet, listen to yourself, it is not your fault.

I've asked myself, how much you commit yourself. It's my life that I cannot forget, it will end one day. Sometimes caught up in a crowd feeling that I do not belong and that people could sense that I was not just a normal man out shopping.

Maybe Davis thought that he could not fit in with society and everyday life, had no personality, and was a broken man. Could not socialise with people of his own age. He would seek attention of children because he would have no friends. You cannot assume your child is safe from this man, sadly there are many out there waiting for their chance to pounce. Most of the times paedophiles are not strangers to you but a likeable friend or even a family member. Do not go into panic mode as it is very unlikely to happen to you. It could be a neighbour, a teacher, a priest, but in my case a football coach.

In many cases child sex abusers suffer from a traumatic experience during their childhood that would be way back in time when it was unheard of. He would suffer in silence until the day he decided to take his own revenge, shame it ended up being me. The system has wised up a lot now but it's still too late for the ones that were abused, thinking they were in a safe environment but end up with a stain or cloud in their memory.

The typical child sex abuser would apply for a job that could give them access to children. There were no real background checks in those days, pass the interview and the job is his. It could be at a school, children's care home for kids that have been neglected by parents that could not cope with them, or even did not want a child in the first place or an accidental pregnancy.

The children that would fall victim, were easy prey, vulnerable and unthreatening to question an adults actions.

He would try to be friendly to gain my family's trust. He would seduce a child with attention, affection and gifts. This is not normal behaviour, I still ask myself why nobody saw right through him to what he was and what he was doing. He would lie and manipulate in a cunning scheme of things, skilfully.

It would be normal for me to depend and trust adults, respect and obey them. As a child who felt loneliness, a little shy, I sure was an easy target for a molester. The abuser would more likely target a child in single parent families, take advantage of the situation. With all this in mind it would be difficult for me to refuse my molester's advances. The vulnerability and opportunity was too hard for him to resist.

I wonder now how he felt when he got home at night with his wicked pleasure still in his mind. Did he cook a meal, go to bed with his thoughts or maybe he relived the night. Maybe he would be calm and content knowing he had got his fix for the night. Like a drug addict that has a craving that they cannot give up. I would have preferred he had done drugs to get over whatever was in his mind. Then children like me would have been safe in thinking this life is good.

It would become obvious that after looking at my private parts at football shower times that I did not complain. If I had said "What are you looking at" he would probably have passed it off as a joke and did not mean anything by it, his get out clause. But I did not say a word. This was wrong of me, but it did not mean much to me at the time. For him though, it was a signal to his warped mind to progress further.

The feeling of guilt is a tough one for me to deal with. Even though what happened was not my fault, I still feel like it was, not good.

I would feel deeply confused as if I enjoyed the attention. As I mentioned earlier it was difficult for me to disclose all this information. I did not understand it until later years into my life. That is when the feelings of feeling dirty, ashamed would become a reality, now knowing I was groomed for it to be the way it was. Maybe it was our lack of knowledge and understanding at the time that gave him his edge or open door to enter?

Look out for the creepy looking guy who hangs about in parks or outside schools. This type of predator would be likely to be caught at some stage but Davis was far too clever for that approach. I suppose the reason parents and family were not aware was because most children will not tell anyone about the abuse for many many years or not at all. For me disclosure was protecting me from having to recall it all again, as you are aware one day it did come back to bite me. I did not display any physical evidence of my abuse, therefore it would not be noticeable, apart from a sore backside that was hidden. Unfortunately for those of us who keep it bottled up inside until later years it can lead to many other things or ailments:-

Difficulty in forming long-term relationships
Depression
Anger
Anxiety
Loss of appetite
Withdrawal from normal activities
Substance abuse
Fear of certain places or people.
Night sweats and panic attacks
Nightmares
Thoughts of suicide
Child sexual abuse can result to mental health problems.

Most of the above happened to me, because I kept my mouth shut, saving everyone else from the pain of knowing about the truth that was mine to keep. I will now tell you a story about a man who was at Hope Springs the same time as me. He was not a victim but an abuser who had broken down once his guilt got the better of him. Not sure why he told me but with me being a victim, of which he did not know, I could easily have lashed out at him. These are some of his words.

"I was a free man with total respect, who would accuse me of wrongdoings, I knew I could get away with it and my word would be the one that was believed. I was a family man, a hardworking man with a sense of responsibility. I also had a happy sex life so I do not understand why I did it."

Yes he would say, *"I sexually abused young boys, I had to confess my sins."*

He would not go into details about how many boys he had entrapped and part of me did not want to know the answer. He would never touch another boy again, he had learned his lesson and deserved the punishment of a flawed man.

It all came to be in the open when one boy was brave enough to speak out. It was to begin an investigation that his family and neighbours took his side and said it is not possible and must be a false allegation from a boy that maybe does not like you.

How could an ordinary man with high moral standards be a child molester? He did not target strangers but ones he had built up a trust with that would never tell. I ended the conversation and would never speak to him again as my blood was boiling and I needed some fresh air. It could be because children would not judge him as an adult would so he may have felt he was doing nothing wrong. I was from a broken home and in his sad sick world he would think he was helping me. He would have his own power and meet his sexual needs, not mine. He would know I could seek support but would be met by a lack of belief, lack of concern and even blame. The truth is this was bad news for me. If it is not dealt with properly at the time, its damaging effects will still be present years later. My groomer was patient, would not want to be caught but at the beginning push to limits that he could see how much he could get away with it. He would present himself in public, be deceptive and be a nice friendly and decent man.

CHAPTER FOURTEEN- SIDE EFFECTS

It is nice now when people meet and greet. It could be a handshake, or a mwah kiss from a distance or furthermore it could be an embracing hug. For a while I could not do any of these, other than to say hello and look down at the ground, trying to hide what I was feeling. Inside your eyes can be a giveaway that something is wrong with me. I started to find it difficult to look at a person eye to eye, I would still talk to them but would not make eye contact. Not sure why but I was hiding something deep inside me.

When I look back upon my life I have felt I was always the one to blame. A sense of shame. It was as if I had sinned without making a confession.

I still have meltdown days when a memory shoots into my mind like a sharp reminder. Lights out, I go to bed, hide under the quilt and try to sleep to make it go away. This happens often as I find myself sleeping for an hour on an afternoon, not because I am tired. I then would wake up not knowing what day it is or what time it is. To even to get me to sleep I started reading the A to Z book which all the possible things a human being can suffer from and ways, means and medications to solve the problem, not a good read. I would then sit in my lounge, of those days, not even to switch the TV on or play music I liked. At the time there was no pleasure for me, I would sooner curl up in a ball and tomorrow would be one of my good days.

I would be invited to family birthday celebrations for a meal and drink but most of the times I made an excuse not to go, I just could not face it. I had to be in the right frame of mind, the right mood, otherwise I felt like I would be too miserable to go and spoil the day. On a good day I could still be the life and soul of the party but that does not happen as much as it used to in my happy days.

The majority of you will not understand why I am reaching

out to you in this book, taboo again, but if you are reading it, maybe you will understand what to hell and back can mean for some of us.

For those of you out there who have had an effect on my life, good and bad, thank you very much? I lost my wife, my home and my career. I really like the ones that have looked out for my health and wellbeing. There are the bad ones, if you are reading this book, will know who you are. Wake up and smell the coffee, do not take me for granted and realise what you have done to a man that did not need any further downers. I am just another human being trying to get on with my life the best I could, with my mask.

A lot has been taken away from me, not through choice, it can be a cruel world and some people do not care as long as they look after number one. I actually pity those people as they will truly not see life for what it really is. A chance to make a difference, welcome people from all walks of life, build up bonds and friendships. Look for the good in people and not the bad. We all have a sad memory inside us but all I can say is value what you have. For me, making another person smile makes my day a better place. To the odd few that are not capable of this, only to have a smile on their faces and not consider the consequences for the type of person they have chosen to be. Everyone can change for the better but for some, I know who you are, I am a good judge of character, at worse maybe you are proud of yourself, god help you.

We ignore our feelings a lot, I realize that. Many of us have to, until they really bite us in the butt. I still have to put a horrible smelly liquid on my finger nails to stop me from biting them. I had resolved in my own mind, the chance to stand face to face with my demons, my truth, the good life lived in a small, various, highly articulate and democratic society.

I am still on the same medication since I was discharged from hospital, a few years now but I am addicted and lose control without them. There are many side effects that one can suffer from but it varies for each individual person. I will list the ones that I have experienced.

Dizziness
Tiredness
Decreased sexual interest
Teeth grinding
Strange dreams or nightmares
Shaking, tremors
Increased sweating

Who in this world would want to know this man again and form a relationship with me? Everything in my life could have been different. It was to be a bad day for me, a week of work with no plans. Staring at four walls, staring out the window, watching rubbish TV and a few beers. Something triggered inside me, telling me there was a painless way to end all of this. My self-respect had gone, my thoughts and feelings were becoming a blur. I stupidly decided not to eat that day to see how I felt, call it my own personal hunger strike, any easy and pointless way to go. I managed to do this for six days, I was very weak, could not stand up on my feet without falling down. It was by chance that I had a family phone call that I admitted what I was doing to myself. Admiration and fair play to my wife and sister. They rushed over and found me curled up in bed, maybe even on my last legs.

An ambulance was called, the paramedics came upstairs to do various tests and they decided that I needed to be in hospital. I had no energy to walk down the stairs so they had to ease me down step by step. I could not even walk to the ambulance so I was put in a wheelchair to get me on board.

At the hospital there was a bed waiting for me so I was put

on various drips and monitors to rehydrate me and give me some liquid food to start with. The odd piece of toast in the morning on my hospital ward was really hard to digest. The amount you eat depends on your stomach. If you have a good appetite you can easily eat and enjoy a good meal. The problem for me, due to lack of food, my stomach had shrunk to the extent that I could only digest small amounts of food until I was well enough to eat a good proper meal. A special thanks has to be said for my sister. She sat there by my bedside the whole night and morning without going to sleep. She was there by my side when I needed it the most. There were to be plenty of vomiting before I was discharged and even had to wait around for four hours because they insisted I saw a specialist before I was allowed to leave.

I still remember my first hospital discharge after my three months in Hope Springs. The feeling of going back to my room for the last time to pack up my belongings. It was like opening the curtains in a dark room, the sunlight shining in. Deep down I knew it was not over and I would return again.
A year later I did have to return to Hope Springs. It was a very bad day for me. I had visited my mother's house and stayed overnight. I slept in the same bed as I did when I lived there as a child. I felt safe but sensed this room was where my first not good memories had come from in my sleep, demons and nightmares I left there the following morning to make my way back home. For various reasons I could not drive my car. I then walked up the road to the bus stop and stood there feeling really sad and lonely, not knowing where I actually belonged. I just felt so isolated from the world with nothing to look forward to.

This was about to be a bad experience. There were two lads waiting at the bus stop, they kept looking at me. Maybe I was being paranoid but I did not feel easy with this situation. Could they see through me and thought I was a loner, see my abuse in my eyes or was just looking for a fight? What I did next was totally wrong.

I went into the shop opposite the bus stop and stole two knives, I was not really sure what I was doing other than to feel a sense of danger. I walked over to the bus stop and waved my knives around, they soon legged it thinking there was a nutter on the loose. My bus arrived and I boarded but still had the knives in my coat pocket. I am not really sure why but I sensed I was in danger again. Re-adjusting to life outside from the hospital was not easy for me.

Like a fool I started to wave my knives around me to the extent that all the other passengers screamed and run of the bus. Believe me this is not the type of person I am here and now. Eventually I was admitted back to Hope Springs but this time not voluntary but under the Mental Health Act. I was seen as a person that could not be safe on the streets. I had no choice, I was taken in as a grade one patient with no privileges. I would scream and scream this time out loud about my abuse. Another two months of my life had gone to waste.

EPILOGUE

I have learnt to communicate again and speak my mind. I have learned how to savour the moment and what I have and not yearn for what I do not have anymore and what I have lost.

I still do really like my ex-wife and stepdaughter but I guess in a different kind of way. We all know that too much has gone on it the past for us to be a real family again, I would have liked that but accept that you cannot turn back the clock and live with my regrets. I have nothing but utter respect for the way they have helped me through my turmoil. When I look back and reminisce, it is hard to believe where I am now. No more suicidal thoughts, no more demons in my mind. But I still beware that once I had been there before there could always be the time that it could come back to haunt me again, so I was told.

The hospital consultant told me that once you have had A.P.E there is a chance it could happen again, touch wood, I think my episode is finally over, but it is not nice living with that thought.

Right now I am trying to be in a place of calm, a place where I can chill out and then handle the chaos of a life better. You don't just get it overnight, you have to work at it. It is a daily struggle but I am winning the battle in my own private way.

If only I understood at the time that it was all wrong. Pride is like a knife, it can cut deep inside. Words are like weapons that wound me sometimes. I feel like I deserved devoted attention, not divided attention. I know I was a bit hyper as a child but many are. I did not deserve what happened to me.

One positive is that I have found something inside me that cares and looks out for people that are having a bad time. Maybe silly but the one day while I was in town I saw a man, a similar age to me, who looked lost. He told me he had been released from a mental health hospital and could not find his way home, he had been in there for many months. I found his ID in his pocket and put him in a taxi with a twenty pound note. I hope someone will do the same for me one day but let's hope it does not come to that.

Child abuse and neglect offend the values of who we really are. As parents we have a responsibility to provide a safe and happy home. It wounds me to confess that I had failed as a child but it made me stronger as an adult but as you know it all came back. In truth I feel bitter and neglected, we now realise that abuse is becoming more common, if only I could see into those people's minds and decide how they became the person they are now. I always thought I had a book inside of me that I would write someday but never expected it to be this *Taboo* one. One thing is for certain, our families are important but why do we neglect that sometimes?

I have learned never to judge a person until you can see through the eyes of that person, like me who had a false mask on and hid my true feelings.

I do not go out and about much these days. I try to limit myself to places I know, familiar and safe. I have this not normal behaviour if I am walking along a busy high street on my own. I cannot cope with people who are too close walking behind me. I either step to one side to let them pass by me or stand in a shop doorway until the pavement is clear.

To conclude I will make a final mention, where I am now and give a little detail to my feelings on the subjects I have mentioned.

Child Abuse: Along with trust issues, which is difficult for me, the hardest part to deal with is the feeling of not being believed, hence it took me many years to speak out about my feelings deep inside me that were protected only by me. I have to live with the scars every day. It matters that I was not even a teenager at the time, sexual abuse is sexual abuse. Some parents or friends cannot accept it because denial is where they would rather stay. I now know who my true friends are, at times of crisis they are the ones that would help me, and others would rather lock the door and close the curtains.

I decided to devote my time, a lot of nights over the last two years to tell my true story, reaching out to you. I have survived, I owe something to anyone who has endured the same pain as me. Isolation and betrayal, I want survivors and children to think they are not alone, let it all out and then have the opportunity to be happy and free from further abuse. It will not be easy, but for me, by doing this I eventually got to the shining light.

Mental Health Hospital: The measure of me as a man, on release from my room and hospital ward is how much I have done and overcome to be the person I am now. I cannot allow myself not to deal with things today, take the day off while the rest of you are fighting your own life to do the best you can, not just for yourself but for your family.

I am now walking in a world that is my own and I can look at myself in the mirror again, it has been a long journey that I would not wish on anyone. Maybe the bravest thing I have ever done was to continue with my life instead of curling up in bed waiting for my death sentence. My emotional black hole is gone, now to be replaced by liking myself again, if you do not like yourself then no one else will, it is a confidence thing. Now I balance my time for when I want to spend time with my family or friends and decide to spend the time on my own, my comfort zone.

Failed Relationships: My marriage was hard to let go of. Sometimes the harder I tried to hold onto it, the more it goes away. I felt so alone, which is hard to explain. There was no point in pretending we had a future together, I was damaged goods, and I would not be the same person again. I will treasure what I had but think we can still be soul mates. I also believe that when we argued it proved how strong we were, to carry on the next day knowing we had voiced our opinions and understood each other better for it. Even though I wanted to move forward in my life I would still have one foot on the brakes. To be free again I had to learn how to let go. Release my hurt, release the fear and refuse to let my past come back to me again. I knew I could no longer make an emotional connection as I know my heart will never be the same again, but I keep telling myself, be strong and I will be OK.

I suppose if I keep looking back at my past and even the present day, I am certain I am going to miss my future. I will fight what is wrong, believe in what is the truth, and do only what is right.

One final comment, your dignity can be mocked, abused, compromised, lower esteem, but it can never be taken away from me. I now have the confidence to reset my boundaries, restore an image I like, start fresh with renewed values and rebuild what has happened to me in the past. I do not feel sorry for myself anymore. I have slammed the door about my past and opened a new door for the present and the future. The devastating effects of sexual abuse do not need to be permanent. I have survived the worst part, the abuse itself, I have choices now that I did not have then.

On a final note while writing my book I have managed to trace Davis. He died in Oswestry, Shropshire, a small market town, in 2009. The death records were there to see. Not sure what I would have done, revenge or forgiveness. It has given me a small peace of mind without ever knowing what he continued to do with his life when he moved on and passed away. Did he go to his grave with his dirty filthy secrets intact? Were there other boys abused that I could have saved if I had spoken out. That I will never know so it does not give me complete closure. On a further final note it seems that his estate went out to the public when he died, which may indicate that his family had broken contact with him or maybe they did find out something about him, at the very least realised what kind of person lurked beneath. I also now know where he was buried but I doubt that I will be visiting with flowers………..

The End

Printed in Great Britain
by Amazon